West Los Angeles Regional Library
Santa Monica Blvd
Los Angeles, CA 90025

W9-BUV-353

JUL 2 8 2003

AUG 1 4 2003

The Library of
NATIVE AMERICANS

The Tongva

of California

Jack S. Williams

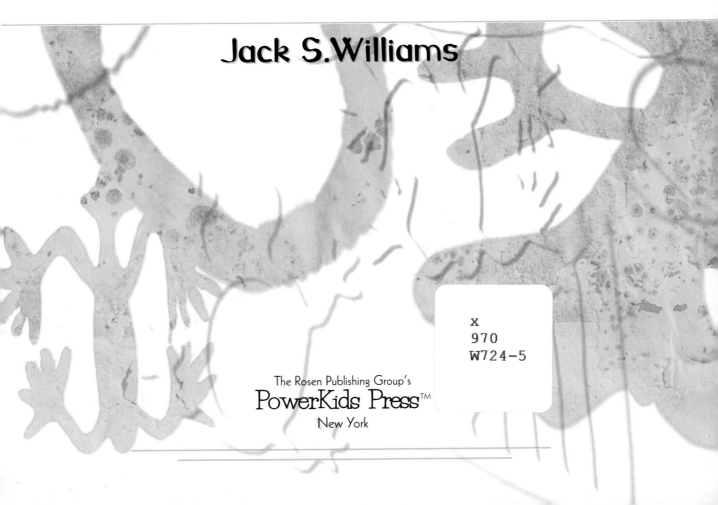

x
970
W724-5

The Rosen Publishing Group's
PowerKids Press™
New York

For my wife, Anita

Published in 2003 by The Rosen Publishing Group, Inc.
29 East 21st Street, New York, NY 10010

Copyright © 2003 by The Rosen Publishing Group, Inc.

All rights reserved. No part of this book may be reproduced in any form without permission in writing from the publisher, except by a reviewer.

Photo and Illustration Credits: Cover and pp. 20, 22, 25, 29 courtesy Anthropology Section, Natural History Museum of Los Angeles County; p. 4 Erica Clendening; p. 7 © Craig Aurness/CORBIS; p. 12 © Joel Sartore/CORBIS; p. 8 © Neil Girling; pp. 10, 16, 19, 26 courtesy Southwest Museum; pp. 15, 31 courtesy Santa Barbara Mission Archive Library; pp. 32, 52, 55 © 2002 Kayte Deioma, all rights reserved; p. 34 © Robert Holmes/CORBIS; pp. 36, 51 © Cristina Taccone; p. 39 © Bettmann/CORBIS; p. 40 courtesy of Mission San Gabriel Arcángel, photo © Cristina Taccone; p. 44 courtesy of Mission San Fernando Rey de España, reproduction photo © Cristina Taccone; pp. 47 and 48 © Photo Collection/Los Angeles Public Library.

Book Design: Erica Clendening

Williams, Jack S.
      The Tongva of California / Jack S. Williams.
            p. cm. — (The library of Native Americans)
      Includes bibliographical references and index.
      ISBN 0-8239-6429-9
      1. Gabrielino Indians—Juvenile literature. I. Title. II. Series.
      E99.G15 W55 2002
      979.4004'9745—dc21

2002002299

Manufactured in the United States of America

There are a variety of terminologies that have been employed when writing about Native Americans. There are sometimes differences between the original language used by a Native American group for certain names or vocabulary and the anglicized or modernized versions of such names or terms. Although this book contains terms that we feel will be most recognizable to our readership, there may also exist synonymous or native words that are preferred by certain speakers.

Contents

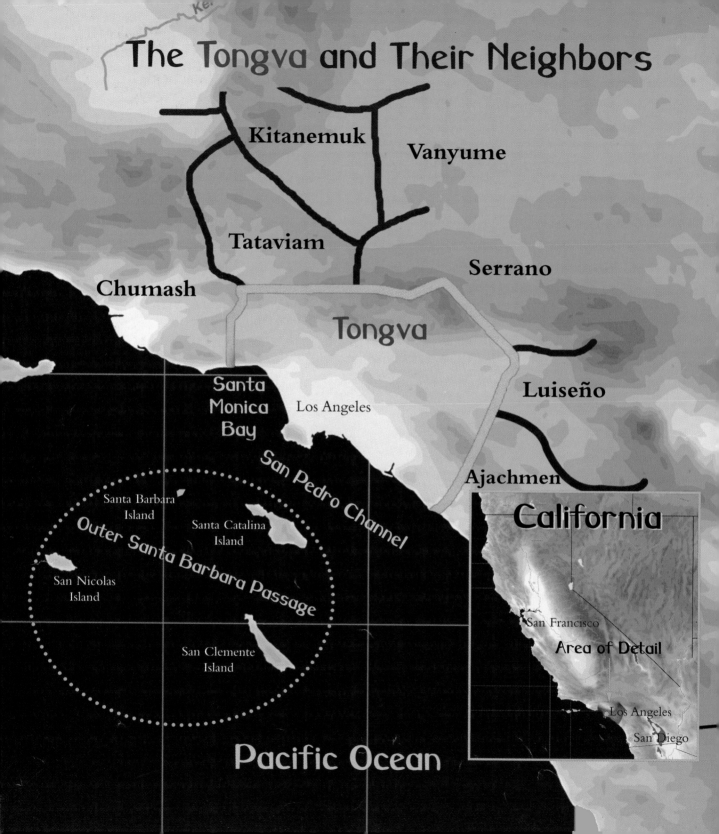

The Tongva and Their Neighbors

Kitanemuk

Vanyume

Tataviam

Serrano

Chumash

Tongva

Santa
Monica
Bay

Los Angeles

Luiseño

San Pedro Channel

Ajachmen

California

Santa Barbara
Island

Santa Catalina
Island

Outer Santa Barbara Passage

San Nicolas
Island

San Francisco

Area of Detail

San Clemente
Island

Los Angeles

San Diego

Pacific Ocean

One

Introducing the Tongva People

Los Angeles is a city of towering skyscrapers and millions of people. Each day its inhabitants race over thousands of miles of superhighways to hundreds of thousands of businesses and homes. Few modern Americans have ever heard about the people who lived in the area that is now Los Angeles more than 200 years ago. If they could turn back the pages of history, they would discover a nation of Native Americans that is known as the Tongva.

Before the first European colonists arrived in 1769, the Tongva inhabited an area that included much of what is today Los Angeles County and northern Orange County. Tongva communities also lived off the coast on San Nicolas, San Clemente, Santa Barbara, and the Santa Catalina Islands. In all, the Tongva nation occupied more than 4,000 square miles.

Experts disagree about how many people lived in the Tongva area. Some believe that there were only 5,000 people. However, others suggest the population may have exceeded 15,000.

The original name of the Tongva has been lost. In the past, they were usually called Gabrieliños, Fernandinos, or Nicoleños, after the names used by the Spaniards for places in the region. Many of

This map shows the locations of the Tongva groups and their neighbors.

the descendants of the natives who lived in these areas prefer to be called the Tongva. The new name is slowly replacing the old ones.

The story of the early Tongva people is one of amazing accomplishments. By using the things that they found in nature, they enjoyed a productive and comfortable way of life. In 1771, their lives were changed forever by the arrival of Europeans, who caused the Tongva to suffer many misfortunes. The Tongvas' experience with the Europeans was filled with conflict. As the decades passed, the Tongva population grew smaller. By 1900, some experts believed that there were no Tongva people left. Today, despite all that has happened, some of the surviving members of the Tongva Nation are working to rebuild their community and to let others know about the fascinating story of their ancestors.

The city of Los Angeles and much of its surrounding urban areas are built on land that has been the homeland of the Tongva for thousands of years.

Two
Origins

Archaeologists are scientists who study the things that ancient people left behind. These objects are known as artifacts. Linguistic anthropologists study how languages develop and spread. By combining the evidence gathered from archaeology and from language studies, we can trace how Native American cultures changed. These cultures changed over time and as a result of living in different places. Researchers use the word culture to indicate a set of shared, learned behavior.

Archaeological evidence suggests that sometime between 13,000 and 40,000 years ago, the ancestors of the Tongva crossed into North America by way of an ice bridge that connected Asia with Alaska. These emigrants began the first colonization of North America.

Experts believe that the history of the Tongva Nation begins with a group of Native Americans who lived in what is now Nevada. Linguistic evidence suggests that this group spoke a variety of the same language, Shoshone, that was spoken by the Tongva. According to the archaeological evidence, these people began to move south and west more than 3,500 years ago. They gradually pushed out, and possibly absorbed, other groups until they reached the shores of the Pacific Ocean. No one can explain why, or how,

Many of the Tongva who lived on California's coastline fished for food and traveled to distant coastal islands in canoes.

they moved. It is not known whether the occupation of other Native Americans' lands by this group was peaceful or violent.

Most experts agree that around 2,500 years ago, the ancestors of the Tongva Nation had made their homes on the coastline of what is now southern California. These Shoshone speakers had already mastered the skills that were needed to harvest the wild foods of the deserts and mountains.

10   The Tongva crafted bowls, stone knives, and many other beautiful objects from the materials they found in their environment. These objects were found on the Channel Islands and were probably made during the late 1700s.

Once they were living on the coast, the ancestors of the Tongva learned how to use the resources found in the ocean. They became expert fishermen and gradually traveled farther and farther away from the shoreline in their canoes. The seafarers eventually brought their families to the distant coastal islands, where they set up new communities. By 500 C.E., the Tongva region included nearly all of the communities that were present when the first Spanish explorers reached California in the sixteenth century. The culture that had emerged among these people would undergo few changes during the next 1,200 years.

Some Native Americans and scholars reject the evidence offered by archaeologists and linguistic anthropologists about the migration of the ancestors of the Tongva Nation. They maintain that the only Native Americans who ever lived in the Los Angeles area were the Tongva.

Three
Daily Life

When European explorers arrived in 1542, they saw the Tongva people for the first time. The explorers were introduced to a way of life that was very different from how they lived in Europe. They saw that the Tongva people wore unique clothes and jewelry, spoke in a different language, believed in their own religion, and built their homes in a different style. What were the daily lives of these Native Americans like?

Living with Nature

The Tongva found almost everything that they needed in nature. They lived in a beautiful land that was filled with many different kinds of resources. The Tongva lived by the Pacific Ocean. The sea provided them with much of their food. Tongva hunters killed dolphins, sea otters, porpoises, seals, and sea lions. Dozens of different kinds of shellfish and hundreds of different kinds of fish ended up in Tongva cooking pots. Native delicacies included bonito, halibut, sardines, sharks, yellowtail, clams, seaweed, and kelp. The plants that the Tongva ate include acorns, cattail pollen, cactus pads, cactus fruit, chia sage seeds, pine nuts, yucca, wild oats, a variety of

The Tongva hunted sea lions that lived along the rocky coastline of California.

berries, and many root crops, such as wild onions and agave hearts. The Tongva hunters brought home snakes, coyotes, antelopes, birds, deer, mountain lions, and rabbits to be eaten. The animals' bodies also provided dozens of other kinds of raw materials, such as fur and bone. Few of the available resources went unused. Even insects, such as grasshoppers, wasps, and caterpillars, were eaten.

Other resources came from the land. The natives used stones and minerals as raw materials for making tools and other products. Trees were an important source of additional raw materials. The Tongva craftspeople preferred to use wood cut from ash, cottonwood, pine, and toyon trees. They also gathered redwood that drifted down the coast from Northern California.

Villages

The Tongva lived in at least two kinds of settlements: large towns and small villages. Much of the population lived in the towns, each of which had as many as 50 houses. Some of the towns had populations of more than 200 people. Other Tongva groups lived in villages, which might not include more than a dozen people. Everyone in the towns lived there year-round, but the smaller communities often moved to other places when food sources in their occupied area dwindled. Experts estimate that there were 50 to 100 Tongva settlements when the first Europeans arrived in the sixteenth century.

The majority of the Tongva lived in small, dome-shaped houses made from wooden poles, brush, and reeds. Most of these single-family homes were about 10 feet (3 m) in diameter. The middle of the room was equipped with a hearth, or fire pit. The flames kept the people warm at night and provided heat for cooking. A hole was left in the center of the roof to allow light to enter and smoke to escape.

Large plank canoes called *ti'at* were built to carry the Tongva on long voyages.

15

The family members slept on reed mats. Some houses were equipped with doors and dividers. Most doorways in the houses of coastal settlements faced the sea in order to avoid the cold winds that sometimes blew down the slopes of nearby mountains.

In the larger settlements on the islands, a similar kind of house was popular. However, these structures were much bigger, measuring as much as 60 feet (18 m) in diameter. Whale ribs were often used in the place of wooden poles. Three or four related families lived in each of these large homes. In the towns on the mainland, the community leaders also had similar houses.

The large villages had special areas used in religious celebrations. The most sacred structure was called the *yuva'r*. It was usually built as an open, oval-shaped enclosure, surrounded with feathers or feathered poles. The Tongva holy men covered

The Tongva prepared food using stone bowls, mortars, and pestles.

the exterior walls with flowers, feathers, and skins. Inside the *yuva'r*, the religious leaders prayed in front of sand paintings and statues of sacred images.

Most villages had sweat lodges. These structures were similar to regular Tongva houses, except that they were partially buried in the ground. A fire was kept burning that filled the room with smoke. The Tongva benefited from sweat lodges in a number of different ways. Sometimes they used sweat lodges for relaxing or bathing, and at other times sweat lodges were used in healing rituals.

Every Tongva settlement had various kinds of coverings made of poles and thatch to provide shade. Reed or brush mats were also planted vertically in the ground to block the wind.

Cooking

The Tongva women were usually in charge of preparing food. They created dishes using many different techniques. Some of the wild plants they ate, such as acorns, had to be ground into powder and washed several times in water to remove toxic acids. The women had to grind or smash some foods such as abalone to make them soft enough to eat. Most of the fruits and berries did not require any preparation.

The natives cooked most of their food outside over an open flame. The Tongva women also knew how to steam or smoke meals. Slabs of soapstone were used as frying pans. Hot rocks were used to cook stews and soups that were prepared in cooking baskets. Other Tongva dishes were made in stone or pottery bowls. Salting, drying, and smoking preserved some of the food, which could then be stored for later use or trade.

Clothing and Body Decoration

The climate of the Tongva region is very mild. As a result, most men and children usually wore no clothing. The women always covered their lower bodies with skirts. Sometimes the Tongva wore capes or blankets. When people had to cross rocky terrain they often put on yucca-fiber sandals. Women sometimes covered their heads with woven hats. Men and women both wore netlike belts. Most of the people decorated their bodies with jewelry, paint, and tattoos. During religious ceremonies, warriors, political leaders, and healers put on dramatic costumes that combined feathers, bones, fur, beads, and seashells. Keeping clean was extremely important to the Tongva. Everyone was expected to take a bath each day.

Arts and Crafts

The Tongva Nation produced beautiful jewelry and useful tools from the natural resources around them. For example, they used stone to make hundreds of different kinds of objects. They chipped

A Tongva woman living during the later part of the nineteenth century wears a traditional hat and holds a basket. The style of clothing was introduced in the missions.

stones to form weapons and tools, such as arrowheads, spear points, knives, scrapers, and drills. The Tongva craftspeople also ground some varieties of stones, such as basalt, granite, and sandstone, into tools, such as pestles, which were shaped like long cylinders. Pestles were used to grind food against mortars, which were large rocks with round holes carved into the tops. Sometimes,

The Tongva made many types of craft objects, such as stone bowls.

holes would be drilled into a large outcropping of stone to create a bedrock mortar. The Tongva women would pass their days sitting on the rocks, grinding nuts and seeds in the holes with pestles as they sang work songs and talked. The nuts and seeds would be reduced to flour in the mortars. The Tongva also made *manos*, which were fist-sized pieces of stone that looked like bars of soap. The *manos* were used with slablike pieces of rock called *metates* to also grind seeds and nuts into flour.

The Tongva used soapstone and serpentine to make arrow-shaft straighteners, cooking bowls, griddles, jewelry, smoking pipes, and doughnut-shaped weights for digging sticks. These types of stone were extremely valuable because they did not crack when they were rapidly heated or cooled. The native craftspeople also used soap-stone and serpentine to make small statues called effigies. Most of the surviving examples of these figurines represent stone birds and sea mammals, such as seals, sea lions, and dolphins.

The Tongva made ceramic pots and jars from clay that they excavated from streambeds and hillsides. After carefully combining the dry clay with water and sand, they formed the mixture into long, cigar-shaped pieces. They coiled these pieces together to form a vessel and smoothed the surface with a round stone and wooden paddle. Once the clay vessels had dried completely, they were stacked together with wood and brush. The stack of pots and fuel was then set on fire. After a few hours of burning, the pottery was allowed to cool. It was then ready to be used. The Tongva did not decorate their ceramic objects. Most of the pots that the crafts-people made were used for cooking. They came in many different sizes and shapes. The potters also made ceramic smoking pipes. Some researchers argue that the Tongva craftspeople did not produce ceramics before the arrival of the Franciscans in 1771. Other experts maintain that the Tongva began making pottery several hundred years earlier.

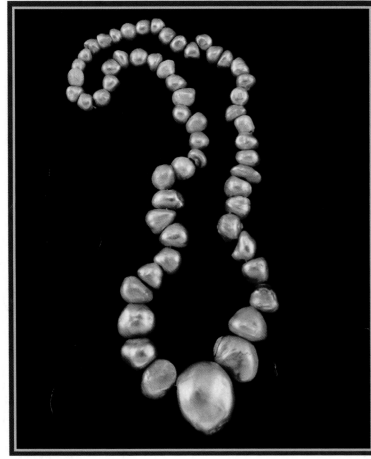

The plant world provided the Tongva with many important raw materials. Tongva women combined cattail, grass, rushes, and willow shoots to make magnificent baskets. By alternating the materials they used, the women were able to decorate the baskets with intricate, geometric patterns. They wove a variety of useful things, including bowls, boxes, buckets, dishes, hats, jars, seed beaters, and trays. The women wove some vessels so tightly that they could hold water. They lined other

The Tongva who lived on the islands created jewelry from the things they gathered from the sea. This necklace is made of abalone pearls.

storage baskets with tar to make them waterproof. The women also used rushes, grasses, and the bark of willow and cottonwood trees to weave skirts.

The Tongva men made items from wood, such as arrows, bowls, canoe paddles, clubs, cups, digging sticks, dishes, jars, house poles, ladles, musical instruments, spoons, stirring sticks, throwing sticks, and trays. The craftspeople used pinesap and tar as glue. Warriors used reeds and thick grasses, such as giant wild rye, to make arrows and knives. The Tongva turned milkweed, agave cactus, and yucca plants into strong strings, cords, and ropes. They also sewed the plant fiber together to make nets, bags, belts, slings, and many other similar objects.

The Tongva made three kinds of boats. The simplest vessels, called dugouts, were made of hollowed-out logs. They also tied reeds, or rushes, tightly together in long bundles to create small vessels called *tule balsas*. Large plank canoes, called *ti'at*, were used for longer voyages. The Tongva seafarers probably adopted the use of these vessels from the nearby Chumash Nation. The Tongva canoes held up to 15 adults. They ranged in length from 12 to 30 feet (3.6–9 m).

The Tongva craftspeople also made many things from the animals they hunted. Women used furs and skins to make clothing and blankets. Animal pelts were boiled to produce a strong glue. Hunters and warriors used rattlesnake venom as a poison for their arrows. Craftspeople transformed bones into beads, combs, gambling sticks, furniture, needles, hairpins, saws, hammers, flutes, panpipes, whistles, and many other tools. Tongva people incorporated feathers into arrows, capes, dance skirts, and headdresses. They transformed seashells into fishhooks, spoons, rattles, scrappers, and knives. The hunters and warriors stripped sinews from the bodies of dead deer and combined these muscles with wood to produce powerful bows. Whale ribs and backbones were even used in house and furniture construction.

Trade

The Tongva were famous for their commercial activities. Their traders used small baskets as standard measures for dry goods, such as seeds. These baskets, which were also worn as hats, were made in one size. The goods were poured into the hats during the exchanges to ensure that the proper amount was changing hands. The Tongva merchants also employed strings of small shell beads as currency. The Tongva who lived on islands traded shell jewelry, dried fish, sea mammal skins, chunks of soapstone, and other soapstone products to Native Americans on the mainland. In return the mainland Native Americans traded deer and rabbit skins, acorns, various nuts and seeds, and other items that were scarce in the islands. Mojave traders from the Colorado River often arrived in the Tongva region with loads of pottery, cotton blankets, and lumps of a red stone called hematite. This stone was used to make paint. The Mojave traders usually exchanged their goods for shell beads, tar, and soapstone.

Social Structure

Social structure is a term used by scholars to describe how some groups of people are divided into smaller units. People in the Tongva Nation belonged to groups based on whether they were men or women, how much wealth they had, how old they were, and who

The grasses and rushes that grew near the Tonga villages were woven into intricately designed baskets.

25

26 This photograph of a Tongva community elder was taken in the late nineteenth
century in San Fernando.

their fathers were. Tongva men enjoyed a great deal of freedom and independence. Although women and girls were usually treated with respect, they had to follow the orders of their husbands, fathers, and brothers.

The smallest Tongva social group was the family. Marriages were not seen as permanent, and husbands often changed wives. Several families were combined to form a clan. The members of a clan shared a common animal ancestor, such as a coyote, an eagle, or a bear. The clans formed into two larger groups, called *moieties*. These organizations helped to regulate trade and other kinds of relations. The largest social group was the village.

The oldest male member of a group was usually its leader. In the villages, the political leaders were called *tumia'r*. Scholars often call these individuals chiefs. Male leaders were allowed to have up to three wives. The villagers usually gave their rulers, and his family, special gifts. The chiefs returned most of these things to the community during religious ceremonies or times of crisis.

Tongva society was also divided into groups based on the amount of wealth they had and the respect that they believed they deserved. The chiefs, their families, and the men who had grown rich through trade, formed the highest rank of this society. Some of the older families and people of above-average wealth formed a middle group. Almost everyone else was considered to be a commoner. Those in the lowest social ranking included war captives or slaves.

Not everyone fit into these social groups. The Tongva had religious leaders who also served as doctors. These individuals spent a great deal of time studying the movement of the stars and planets in the night skies. They also collected sacred objects that were thought to be filled with various kinds of supernatural powers. These religious healers were widely respected, and often were feared by their enemies. Most Tongva people believed that the powers that these religious people possessed could be used for either good or evil. Most of these religious leaders were men.

Government

The Tongva's basic unit of government was the village or town. The *tumia'r*, or chief, ruled the community. He was responsible for settling disputes within the settlement, making collective decisions, leading his people in war, and planning most religious ceremonies. You became a *tumia'r* because your father was a *tumia'r*. When a family did not produce a son, a daughter was sometimes allowed to become a political or religious leader. Family members aided most chiefs by working for them as messengers, tax collectors, and advisers.

The Tongva village leaders sometimes formed temporary alliances. A single chief could rule the combined communities. Every village had its own territory. Anyone who tried to hunt or gather food in these areas without permission could be attacked.

Warfare

The Tongva went to war for many different reasons. Sometimes they fought to defend themselves against outsiders. They also fought other Tongva villages over territory or for revenge. When they went to war, the *tumia'r* led the young men into battle. The old men, women, and children carried the supplies that the fighters needed. The warriors' favorite weapons were bows and arrows, spears, and clubs. Some of the fighters wore body armor made of reeds.

The purpose of their attacks was usually to destroy their enemies. Sometimes the victorious army carried off captive women

These knife and harpoon points were used by the Tongva to hunt for food.

and children to become slaves. Captured men were usually executed in a village ceremony. The warriors also raided enemy villages for plunder or to capture women.

Language

The Tongva spoke a language that belongs to the Shoshone branch of the Uto-Aztecan language group. At least four different dialects, or regional variations, of the language were spoken. Tongva speakers could have probably easily recognized where a person was born based on the dialect that he or she spoke.

Religion

The Tongva people's lives were deeply intertwined with their religion. Their faith helped them to make sense of the world and figure out what they needed to do to be good people.

The Tongva way of looking at the structure of the universe was very different from that of most modern Americans. For example, according to some elders, a supreme being called Qua-o-ar, or Chingichngish, organized the universe by laying it out on the shoulders of seven giants.

One of the most important stories of the Tongva involved the appearance of Qua-o-ar. Some elders said the heavens and Earth were originally brother and sister. They worked together through six different creations before they produced the present world. Earth then gave birth to Wiyot, who ruled the Tongva but who was very cruel. Wiyot's sons finally killed him to put an end to his bad behavior. As the Tongva people came together to decide what to do next, they had a sudden vision of a ghostlike being who called himself Qua-o-ar. He told the people that he had come to rule them and furnish them with good laws. After choosing the groups that would

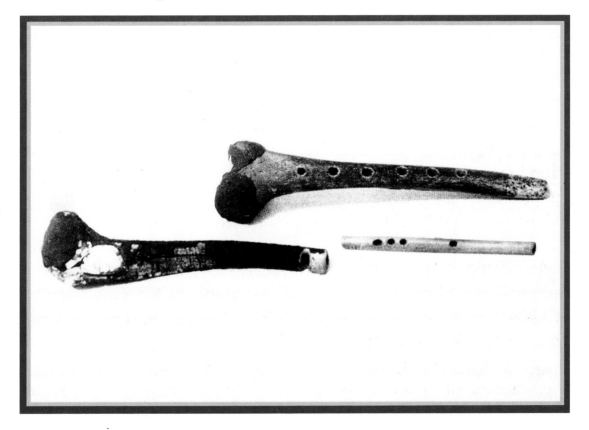

The Tongva created musical instruments from bone.

31

provide political and spiritual leadership, the god began to dance and slowly rose into heaven.

Most of the Tongva holidays involved worship. Their calendar was filled with religious rituals that traced the path of a person from birth to death. Funeral services were particularly important. Other groups of celebrations marked the passing seasons. Many of the religious services emphasized the need to balance the powers that existed in the universe. Sickness, death, and destruction could result if these powers fell out of balance.

This is a modern copy of images that the Tongva once painted or scratched into rock.

The Tongva's religious rituals usually involved songs and dances. Voices, flutes, rattles, and whistles provided the music. Split pieces of wood, called clapper sticks, were used to snap out a rhythm. Tongva craftspeople tied a piece of wood or stone to the end of a string to make a bullroarer. When the musician spun the bullroarer in the air, it hummed loudly. The men usually performed the sacred dances. The women participated by singing. The religious leaders wore special clothing and paint that made them look like animals or supernatural beings.

Tongva people sometimes marked the surface of rocky outcropping with symbols or other markings. The product of their efforts is known as rock art. Sometimes they used paint to mark the rocks. These pictures are called pictographs. Other symbols were created by scratching away some of the rocks' outer surface. This kind of picture is called a petroglyph. The Tongva also created complex designs using colored sand. This kind of work is known as sand painting. We do not know why the Native Americans made rock art or sand paintings. Many scholars think that these images were made during religious rituals. Because rock art and sand painting are sacred to many modern Native Americans, it is very important that people show respect when they view them.

Four
Coping with Newcomers
(1542–1900)

In 1542, Juan Rodriguez Cabrillo became the first European to contact the Tongva. When he discovered the natives living on San Pedro and Santa Catalina Islands, he found them to be friendly and interested in trade. As he sailed northward, he encountered other Native Americans who attacked his men. In a conflict, Cabrillo was wounded and later died. His men returned to Mexico and told everyone that there was nothing of value in California.

During the 200 years that followed, other Spanish ships visited California. Tongva people probably met with many of the ships' crews, and might have even traded with them. Although we lack precise records about this period, it is extremely likely that European diseases, such as smallpox and measles, killed many Native Americans in California, just as they had killed large numbers of Native Americans in other parts of the continent. By the time that the Spanish Empire launched an expedition to occupy California in 1769, the Tongva nation had probably suffered a dramatic drop in its population and was gradually restoring its numbers.

This monument in San Diego depicts explorer Juan Rodriguez Cabrillo. He was the first European to encounter the Tongva.

The Tongva and the Missions

During the middle of the eighteenth century, the king of Spain began to worry about the growing number of British and Russian ships in the Pacific Ocean. He soon became afraid that some other nation might occupy California. An expedition was sent to absorb the region into the Spanish Empire in 1769. Two years later, a mission was established at San Gabriel. Why did Spain decide to build a mission?

Carlos III, king of Spain, wanted to conquer California. However, he did not have the colonists, the money, or the soldiers that he needed to do this. He thought that he could defeat his rivals by recruiting Native Americans to help him defend the

The Mission Church of San Gabriel was created to teach the Tongva about Christianity and European customs.

region. Government officials decided that they would use missions as outposts to form a series of alliances with some of the native people of California. Similar outposts had been used in other frontier areas as a way of making peace with Native Americans. The Spanish government decided to place Junípero Serra, a Franciscan priest, in charge of the missions.

Father Serra was delighted to head the new operation. He believed that the creation of the missions would provide an opportunity for him to perform his patriotic duty and share his religion. Europeans did not understand that most of the Tongva and other natives of California considered themselves to be wealthy, powerful, and happy. Because the natives' lifestyle was different than that of Europeans, Serra saw them as poor people who needed to be helped. He and many other missionaries loved poor people. They thought that God especially blessed the poor. The missionaries wanted to create a kind of community that would combine the best of the Spanish and Native American worlds. Most of all, Serra and his followers wanted to create a society where there would be social justice for the poor. To create this community, they believed that the Native Americans had to become Roman Catholics.

The missions were designed to do many different things. On one hand, they were centers of religious instruction. However, they were also communities in which many European trades and customs were taught. Most of all, they were outposts of the Spanish Empire where the government worked with Native Americans toward common goals. These missions would bring many changes to the region's Native Americans.

The success of Spain's California colony depended on the missionaries' ability to get natives to live and work in the new Franciscan settlements. Why would a Tongva person want to live in a mission? When the priests came, they offered the Native Americans a number of practical things. The Spanish soldiers' powerful cannons, firearms, steel swords, steel-tipped spears, and leather armors impressed the Tongva warriors. The Tongva concluded that these foreigners would make better friends than enemies. Many Tongva people also liked the other European things they saw, such as glass beads, steel knives, axes, dozens of new kinds of food, and amazing animals. They realized that they could accumulate wealth by trading these things to other Native American groups. The strange men wearing gray robes also offered the Tongva many beautiful things that they had never seen, including paintings, statues, new religious rituals, and powerful music.

It is also clear that some of the Tongva were caught up in the excitement of the Franciscans' preaching. The priests offered the Native Americans a vision of utopia, or a perfect world, in which everyone lived a happy, useful life. Today we recognize that no one has ever been able to build such a utopia. The Native Americans who had the least power and wealth in the Tongva community were probably the most attracted to the missionaries' vision.

Padre Junipero Serra.
Founder of the California Missions.
S-615

The government of Spain put the Franciscan priest Junípero Serra in charge of the missions in California.

39

Some of the Tongva decided that they wanted to live in the missions and become neophytes, or new followers. Several Tongva chiefs moved whole villages of people to the new outpost at San Gabriel. These leaders continued to serve as the officials of the new town. Many other individual Native Americans also moved to the missions. The Franciscan priests functioned as special governors for the Christian Tongva. The priests worked closely with a council made up of the traditional leaders. The missionaries maintained peace between all the different communities that lived together at the mission. Although they made their permanent home at the Franciscan settlement, the neophytes regularly visited the non-Christian Tongva people, whom the

First Adult Indian Baptismo
performed by
Fr. Junipero Serra
1778

This document from Mission San Gabriel records the first baptism of a Native American. It was performed by Junípero Serra in 1778.

Spanish called gentiles. By giving the Christian Native Americans the freedom to travel throughout the region, the Franciscans were able to find new natives for the mission.

Not all of the Tongva thought that the missions were a good idea. They were suspicious of the gifts that the Europeans offered. Most of the people at the missions thought that they would be able to keep both their own traditional ways and those of the newcomers. The people who opposed the missions recognized that, over time, they would change the Tongva into something new and different. It soon became obvious that there was no place in the new community for the old Tongva faith. Many traditional Native American religious leaders grew to hate the Franciscans. Although most of the people who chose to live in the missions appeared to have enjoyed their new lives, a small number ran away and joined forces with the other Native Americans who opposed the newcomers. Some of the people who did not join the missions simply avoided all contact with them.

The history of Mission San Gabriel is not a happy one. During the first ten years, the Franciscans and their Native American followers suffered through many difficult days. There were a number of battles fought between the Tongva warriors and the Spanish soldiers who were assigned to protect the mission. In one of these conflicts, the soldiers started trouble with the Native Americans, cruelly attacking one of the Tongva women. The priests and the Native Americans demanded that the governor of California punish the troops. As soon as the fighting was over, San Gabriel was hit by another disaster. Floods washed away the first mission buildings and a new settlement had to be created some distance away. Despite these setbacks, more and more Tongva people answered the call of the mission bells. By 1778, most of the people of the nearby villages had moved to San Gabriel.

Some Tongva people liked the things that the Europeans brought but did not want to live at the Franciscan outpost. Some of these gentiles worked for the Spanish settlers who lived in Los Angeles, which was established in 1781.

The religious leaders of the old Tongva faith grew angrier as the numbers of their followers steadily declined, along with the size of the Tongva territory. One of the most remarkable people of the era was a Native American holy woman named Toypurina. Her life reflects just how complicated it was for the Tongva to live alongside the newcomers.

Toypurina was ten years old when the Spaniards first arrived to establish Mission San Gabriel. As she grew up, Toypurina became an important religious leader to those who believed in the ancient Tongva faith. In 1785, when she was twenty-four years old, she formed an alliance with some of the unhappy neophytes to kill the priests and destroy the mission. The soldiers discovered her plans and she was arrested. At her trial, Toypurina stated that she opposed the Franciscans because they were stealing her people's land. After she was found guilty, Toypurina was sent into exile at Mission San Carlos Borroméo, near Monterey. The people who lived there accepted Toypurina as a member of their community. Eventually she became a Christian and fell in love with one of the soldiers who guarded the mission. After they were married, Toypurina moved to the Presidio of Monterey, the military base that was also the capital of California. When her husband was assigned to guard the new mission at San Juan Bautista, she moved with him to the outpost. Toypurina died of natural causes as a member of the Spanish, and not the Native American, community. She gave birth to four children. One of her sons became a soldier and one of her daughters married a soldier.

When Toypurina's revolt failed in 1785, conditions worsened for both the Christian Native Americans and the Franciscans living in the Tongva region. New restrictions were placed on Native American travel. A series of raids by hostile gentiles drove off many of the town's and mission's animals. For a while, it looked as if the Native American warriors might bring an end to the Spanish settlements. However, conditions soon quieted, and new people began to move into the mission.

By 1790, there were new challenges for the remaining Tongva gentiles. Spain did not control the islands to the west of California. After 1790, other nations' ships freely visited the islands of Santa Barbara, Santa Catalina, San Clemente, and San Nicolas. Parties of Russians and their Native American Inuit allies ventured south to hunt sea otters and seals. When they reached the Tongva villages on the islands, they sometimes traded with the natives. However, violence often broke out. During the next 40 years, a series of smugglers, whalers, and other foreigners used the islands. The Tongva who lived there were gradually killed off or were driven to the mainland.

In 1797, a new mission was established at San Fernando. The Franciscans wanted to recruit the remaining northern Tongva. Many of these natives worked for the settlers in Los Angeles. They had already adopted numerous foreign customs, such as farming and living in Spanish-style buildings.

Modern actors at Mission San Fernando portray Native Americas making adobe bricks.

By 1800, the remaining Tongva recognized that the newcomers could not be ignored. During the past twenty-five years, the small herds of horses, sheep, and cattle that had been brought to California by the missionaries and settlers had steadily grown. As their numbers increased, they ate more and more of the plants that the Tongva relied on for food. The animals also disrupted many other features of the area's ecology. For example, they sometimes ate all of the grasses covering a hillside, which allowed the winter rains to carry away the soil and cause a landslide. Epidemic diseases that had been introduced from Europe continued to kill both Tongva neophytes and gentiles. It was now almost impossible for the Tongva people to live in a traditional way. Some of the remaining gentiles finally gave up and moved into the missions. A small number of Tongva led secret lives in the rugged mountains and canyons. Other Tongva joined with Native American tribes that lived to the northeast, in California's immense central valley. Occasionally, they returned to raid the Spanish settlements.

The number and strength of the attacks against the missions gradually grew. In 1810, a force described by some to have included 800 mounted Native American warriors assaulted Mission San Gabriel and captured 3,000 sheep. The raiders departed the outpost at the same lightening speed with which they had struck. They left the buildings of the mission unharmed and the population untouched. The Spanish troops from the military base at Santa Barbara were able to reclaim the sheep and capture some of the mission's opponents. Most of the hostile Tongva warriors and their allies escaped.

After 1810, a new threat appeared on the horizon. Mounted Mojave raiders, who lived along the banks of the Colorado River, began to attack the Tongva and their Spanish allies. The Mojave had always come to the Tongva area to trade. Now they came to steal horses, mules, cattle, and slaves. In 1819, the Spanish built an elaborate mission ranch protected by a defensive wall at San Bernardino. Many of the gentile Tongva people who remained on the eastern edge of the frontier joined the new community for protection. However, the Mojave continued to strike fear in the hearts of their enemies. In 1821, the problems with the desert raiders had become so bad that the governor of California ordered that tall walls be built to help defend Mission San Fernando and Mission San Gabriel.

Despite the troubles, the number of Tongva residing at the missions continued to grow. When large-scale trade between foreign merchants and Spanish settlements began around 1810, there was a dramatic increase in the amount of wealth that was available to the Franciscans. The combination of money and Native American workers made it possible for the missions to become major frontier outposts. The neophytes now lived in comfortable homes that were similar to those found in settlements built by the Europeans, in areas such as Los Angeles and Santa Barbara. The communities included magnificent churches, fountains, aqueducts, warehouses,

El Pueblo de Los Angeles
1781

North

PLAZA

H   I   J   K

ALLEY

G
F

ALLEY

E
D

C B A

ALLEY

L
M

ALLEY

N
O

P

ZANJA OR WATER-DITCH FROM LOS ANGELES RIVER

Marchessault St.

Founded 1780

Camino Real to San Gabriel

Plan of the Original Spanish Pueblo de Los Angeles

A	Town House	I	House Lot of Expelled Settler
B	Guard House	J	" " " "
C	Public Grain House	K	" " " Bacillio Rosas
D	House Lot of Pablo Rodriguez	L	" " " Alejandro Rosas
E	" " Jose Vanegas	M	" " " Vacant
F	" " Jose Moreno	N	" " Antonio Navarro
G	" " Antº Valarieneio	O	" " Manl Camero
H	" " Expelled Settler		

The Plaza was 280 Ft x 210 Ft in Size
Lots D. E. F. G. L. M. N. O. were 55 x 111 feet
The north west corner of the old Plaza of today forms the location of the original Plaza
at the south east corner at P.

To be perfected and engraved
for my Annals of Los Angeles

This document shows the plan for the original Spanish settlement of Los Angeles in 1781.

47

factories, workshops, and many elaborate buildings. The neophytes learned the skills of farming and cattle raising, and they mastered many other European trades and arts. There was more than enough food and there were trade goods enough to satisfy the needs and desires of the Tongva missions' population.

Even though the Franciscan settlements looked increasingly like prosperous towns, there were still many serious problems in the settlements. Some of the Native Americans did not feel that they

This picture was taken in 1859 and is one of the earliest photographs of Los Angeles.

were being treated fairly by the newcomers. Many Spanish settlers tried to cheat their native employees. Diseases continued to kill off more Native Americans each year than were born. Working together, the Tongva leaders and the Franciscans managed to cope with the problems. Most Christian natives seem to have believed that they had a future as a Native American community in a white world.

In 1822, the Tongva learned that Spain had abandoned its claim to California and that Mexico had claimed the area. They were now citizens of Mexico. The republic's officials promised the Tongva neophytes that they would receive complete control of their towns and all the other mission property. Most of the Native Americans at the missions believed that they were ready to govern themselves as equal citizens of the new nation.

The promises of a better future grew dim as a series of delays prevented the Mexican government from completing its plan to end the missions. The attacks from the Mojave continued. The neophytes and the Spaniards also had to fight off new raids by mounted Yokuts warriors from the north. The Native Americans of the central valley of California had expanded their attacks as they found new markets for stolen horses and mules. After 1830, traders from New Mexico arrived in the Yokuts' territory. They were eager to exchange blankets and other items for stolen animals.

Between 1833 and 1835, the final act in the story of the missions took place. The populations of San Gabriel and San Fernando dwindled as Mexican officials moved to eliminate the missions. The government promises were never fulfilled. Instead the Mexican settlers from Los Angeles took almost everything that the Tongva people who lived at the missions had worked so hard to create and defend.

The Tongva Between 1834 and 1900

The elimination of the missions was especially devastating for the Tongva. The new economic boom seen in Los Angeles and the surrounding ranches overwhelmed what remained of the mission communities. Most Tongva appear to have taken up jobs working for wealthy Mexican ranchers or townspeople. Enemy Native American groups from the north and the east, along with Mexicans, attacked any remnants of the traditional Tongva population. It became clear that there were no places where the refugees could go. The Tongva Nation were a people without a homeland.

In 1850, when California became a U.S. state, the new government did nothing to improve the situation for the Tongva. Diseases, discrimination, and poverty brought an early end to the lives of many of the mission survivors. After the United States took over California in 1848, a few dozen individuals living in the traditional way continued to cling to survival in what had once been eastern Tongva territory. By 1900, very few people, including the Tongva, identified themselves as descendants of the mission Native Americans. It seemed to many Los Angeles residents that the Tongva had vanished.

Today Mission San Fernando contains many artifacts that show the history of the Tongva.

Five

The Tongva Today

Despite their plight in the eighteenth and nineteenth centuries, the first nation of Los Angeles has survived. No one is sure exactly how many members of this ancient Native American group remain. Experts have estimated that the population ranges in size from a few hundred to a few thousand. It is hard to get an accurate count because, unlike many of the other California Native Americans, the Tongva do not have a reservation. Individuals from the Tongva community have been particularly active in the environmental movement. They want to save the parts of their traditional lands that have not been turned into modern cities. Tongva people have also fought against government agencies to save those places sacred to the Tongva and for the right to revive Tongva religious customs. They are working hard to preserve all of their surviving traditions. They continue their long struggle for justice.

One of the modern Tongva leaders who is trying to make a difference is Martin Alcala. In 2001, he was the chair of the Gabrieliño/Tongva Indians in west Los Angeles. Although these Native Americans have not been recognized by the U.S. government, Alcala and others have been working hard to find appropriate places to store the religious things that have been taken

Joseph Ontiveros helps to preserve ancient Tongva traditions by serving as the curator of the Haramokngna Cultural Center at the Angeles National Forest in Arcadia, California. This photograph was taken during the Winter Solstice ceremony.

from Tongva sacred places. They look forward to the day when Native Americans will determine how, and where, these items will be seen.

Today much of the natural world that the ancient Tongva lived in has vanished. Some of the names of places they lived in are still being used, including Tujunga, Cucamonga, and Topanga. Magnificent Tongva artifacts and artwork can be seen in a number of important museums in the United States and Europe. The Tongva missions at San Fernando and San Gabriel, which are now museums, also share evidence of the Tongvas' importance and their tragic encounter with outsiders. Despite all the challenges that they have faced, the Tongva are still with us. They represent a courageous people who are an important part of our nation's heritage.

These are modern versions of traditional Tongva musical instruments. They include clapper sticks and a leather rattle decorated with symbols found in Tongva rock art.

55

Timeline

13,000–40,000 years ago	The ancestors of the Tongva arrive in North America from Asia.
6,000–8,000 years ago	Native Americans occupied the area later inhabited by the Tongva Nation.
3,500 years ago	Most scholars believe that the Shoshone speakers, who are the ancestors of the Tongva, begin the long migration to the south and the west.
2,500 years ago	Most scholars believe that Shoshone speakers arrive on the coast of southern California. These people are probably the ancestors of the later Tongva Nation.
500 years ago	Most scholars believe that the way of life recorded in 1542 by the Spaniards had been adopted by the Tongva. This way of life continued until the arrival of the first Spanish colonists in 1769.
1542	Juan Rodriguez Cabrillo reaches the Tongva area and claims it for Spain.

1769	The first Spanish colonists invade California.
1771	The first mission for the Tongva is established at San Gabriel.
1797	The second mission for the Tongva is established at San Fernando.
1821	Mexico becomes independent of Spain.
1833–1835	The missions are eliminated by the order of the Mexican government. Within a few years virtually all the native peoples' property was stolen by non-Native Americans.
1846–1848	The United States conquers California. Native Americans lose many civil rights under the new government.
1850–1900	During this period, the surviving members of the Tongva Nation suffer intense discrimination and persecution. Some experts mistakenly claim that no Tongva are left after 1900.
1924	All Native Americans are made U.S. citizens.
1960–present	Some Tongva begin to rebuild their community and seek tribal recognition by the U.S. government.

Glossary and Pronunciation Guide

anthropologists (an-thruh-PAH-luh-jists) Scholars who study the physical, social and cultural aspects of human life.

aqueduct (AH-kwuh-dukt) A humanmade channel used to carry water.

archaeologists (ar-kee-AH-luh-jists) Scientists who study ancient people's behavior through the objects that they left behind.

artifact (AR-tih-fakt) Any object showing evidence of human activity.

bedrock mortar (BED-rok MOR-tur) A rock with carved holes that is used to grind seed and nuts into flour.

chief (CHEEF) A leader who possesses special privileges and guides his people in war, plans religious ceremonies, and settles disputes.

clans (KLANZ) A group of families that claim to be related to the same animal ancestor.

culture (KUHL-chur) Shared, learned behavior.

dugout (DUG-out) A kind of canoe made by hollowing out a log.

effigies (EH-fih-jeez) Three-dimensional models of living things.

Gabrieliños (gab-ree-oh-LEEN-yohs) A name used for the Tongva of Mission San Gabriel.

Fernandinos (fer-nan-DEEN-ohs) A name used for the Tongva of Mission San Fernando.

gentile (JEN-tyl) A word used by missionaries to identify non-Christian Native Americans.

hearth (HARTH) A pit used for fires.

hematite (HEE-mah-tyt) A mineral that can be used to make red paint.

linguistic anthropologist (lin-GWIHS-tik an-thruh-PAH-luh-jist) A scholar of anthropology who focuses on the study of language.

manos (MAH-nohs) Fist-sized pieces of stone used to grind seeds on a metate.

metates (me-TOH-tays) Stone slabs with a bowl-like depression used with a mano.

mission (MIH-shun) In colonial California, a kind of Spanish settlement where Native Americans were to be transformed into Christian citizens.

moiety (MOY-at-tee) A kind of social unit that divides a community into two groups, based on family relationships.

mortars (MOR-turz) Rocks with circular holes that were used to crack nuts and grind seeds into flour.

neophytes (NEE-uh-fyts) A term used for mission Native Americans who lived under Spanish rule.

Nicoleños (nick-oh-LEEN-nyohs) A name used for the Tongva of San Nicolas Island.

pendants (PEN-duhnts) A type of jewelry suspended on a cord worn around the neck.

pestles (PES-tuhlz) Cylindrical-shaped pieces of rocks used with mortars.

petroglyphs (PEH-truh-glifs) Rock art that is created by scratching the outer surface off of rocks.

pictographs (PIK-toh-grafts) Rock art that is created by painting images onto rock surfaces.

Qua-o-ar or Chingichngish (KWAY-oh-are or CHING-echn-gash) An important Tongva god.

rock art (ROK ART) An art tradition that involves painting and scratching decorations and symbols on the surface of rocks.

serpentine (SUR-puhnt-een) A kind of stone, similar to soapstone, used to make jewelry and tools.

sinew (SIN-yoo) A muscle.

soapstone (SOHP-stohn) A soft stone used to make cooking utensils, beads, and other tools.

social structure (SOH-shul STRUHK-chur) A way of dividing a community into different groups of people.

ti'at (TEE-aht) A kind of Tongva canoe made out of planks.

Tongva (TOHNG-va) The modern name for the Shoshone-speaking Native Americans who traditionally lived in the Los Angeles basin and adjacent islands.

tule balsa (TOO-lee BAWL-saw) A kind of canoe made from bundles of reeds.

tumia'r (TOO-me-ah-or) A Tongva village leader or chief.

utopia (yoo-TOH-pee-uh) A perfect community in which everyone is treated fairly and is happy.

yuva'r (YOU-vah-or) A Tongva structure in which religious leaders prayed and religious celebrations were held.

Resources

BOOKS

Campbell, Paul D. *Survival Skills of Native California*. Salt Lake City, UT: Gibbs Smith, 1999.

Engelhardt, Zephyrin. *San Gabriel Mission and the Beginnings of Los Angeles*. San Gabriel, CA: Mission San Gabriel, 1927.

Johnston, Bernice Eastman. *California's Gabrieliño Indians*. Los Angeles, CA: Southwest Museum, 1962.

Malinowski, Sharon, ed. *Gale Encyclopedia of Native American Tribes*. Detroit, MI: Gale Group, 1998.

Miller, Bruce W. *The Gabrieliño*. Los Osos, CA: Sand River Press, 1991.

Rawls, James J. *Indians of California: The Changing Image*. Norman, OK: University of Oklahoma Press, 1986.

Stanley, Terry. *Digger: The Tragic Fate of the California Indians from the Missions to the Gold Rush*. New York: Crown Publishing/ Random House, 1997.

MUSEUMS

Natural History Museum of Los Angeles County
900 Exposition Boulevard
Los Angeles, CA 90007
Web site: http://www.nhm.org
The NHM houses important collections of Tongva artifacts.

Southwest Museum
234 Museum Drive
Los Angeles, CA 90065
Web site: http://www.southwestmuseum.org
The museum preserves major collections of Tongva artifacts and photographs of later Tongva people.

MISSIONS

Mission San Fernando
15151 San Fernando Mission Boulevard
Mission Hills, CA 93145-1109

Mission San Gabriel
428 South Mission Drive
San Gabriel, CA 91776
Web site: http://www.sangabrielmission.org

WEB SITE

Tribal Home of the Gabrieliño/Tongva Nation
http://www.tongva.com/lands.htm
This is the official Web page of the Tongva. It is an informative place to begin your own Tongva research.

Index